Welcome to *Naturescapes: A Coloring Experience for Nature Lovers*

Within this book exists the magic we may find in nature if we choose to see it. The sun's warm embrace, a dragonfly's dance, a flower's journey, and a mountain's layers-- all works of art to keep us inspired and grateful. Please, keep looking.

Test Your Materials Here

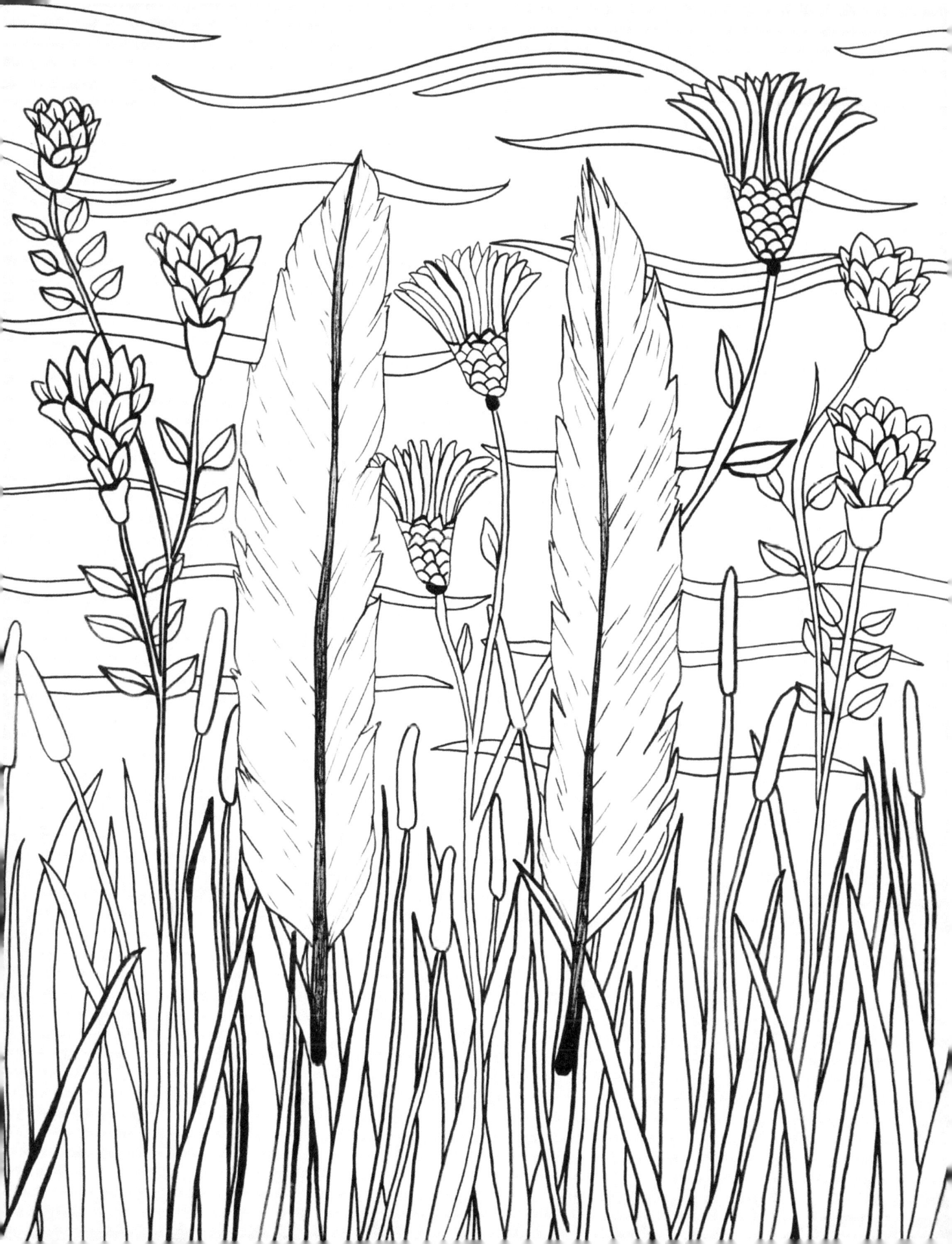

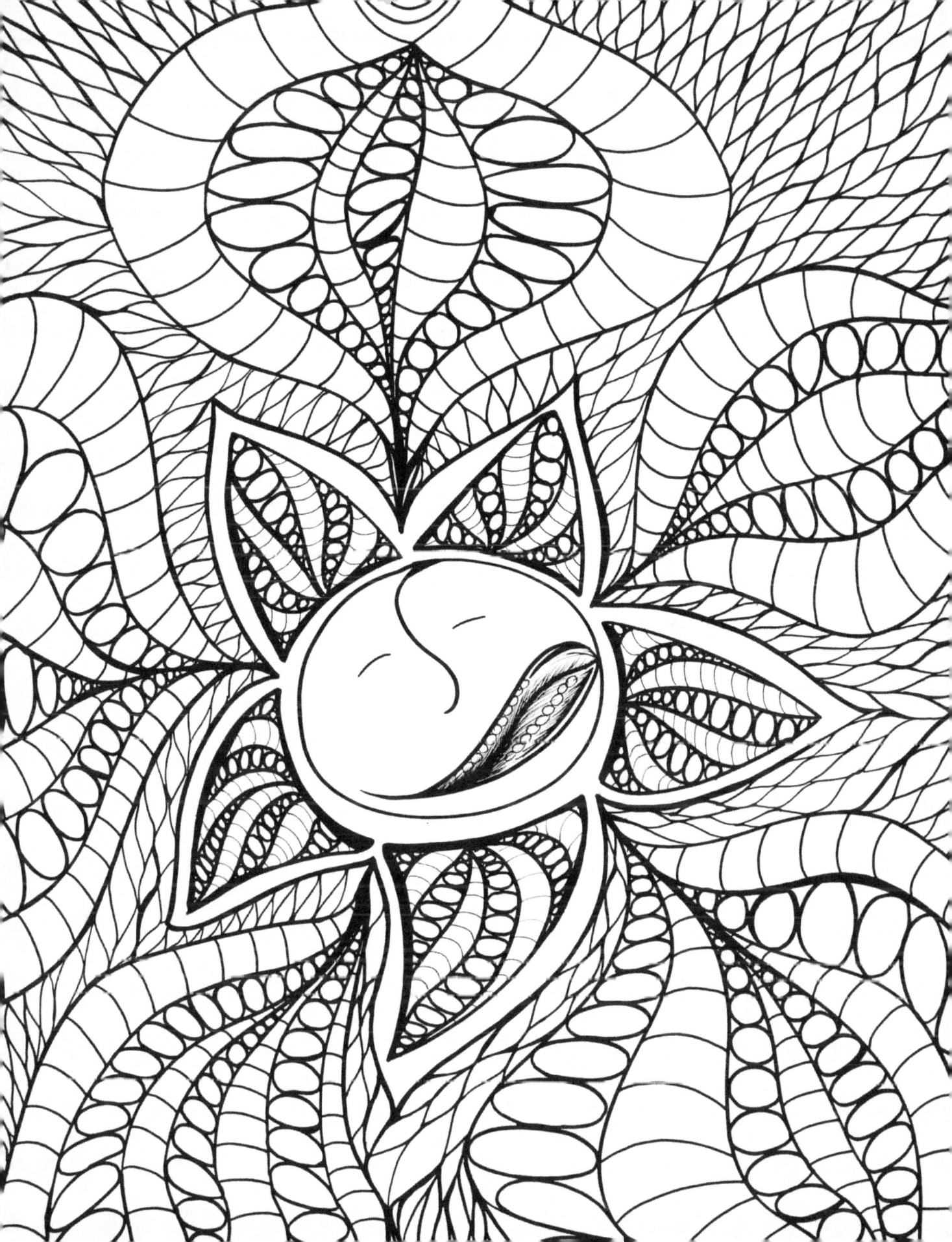

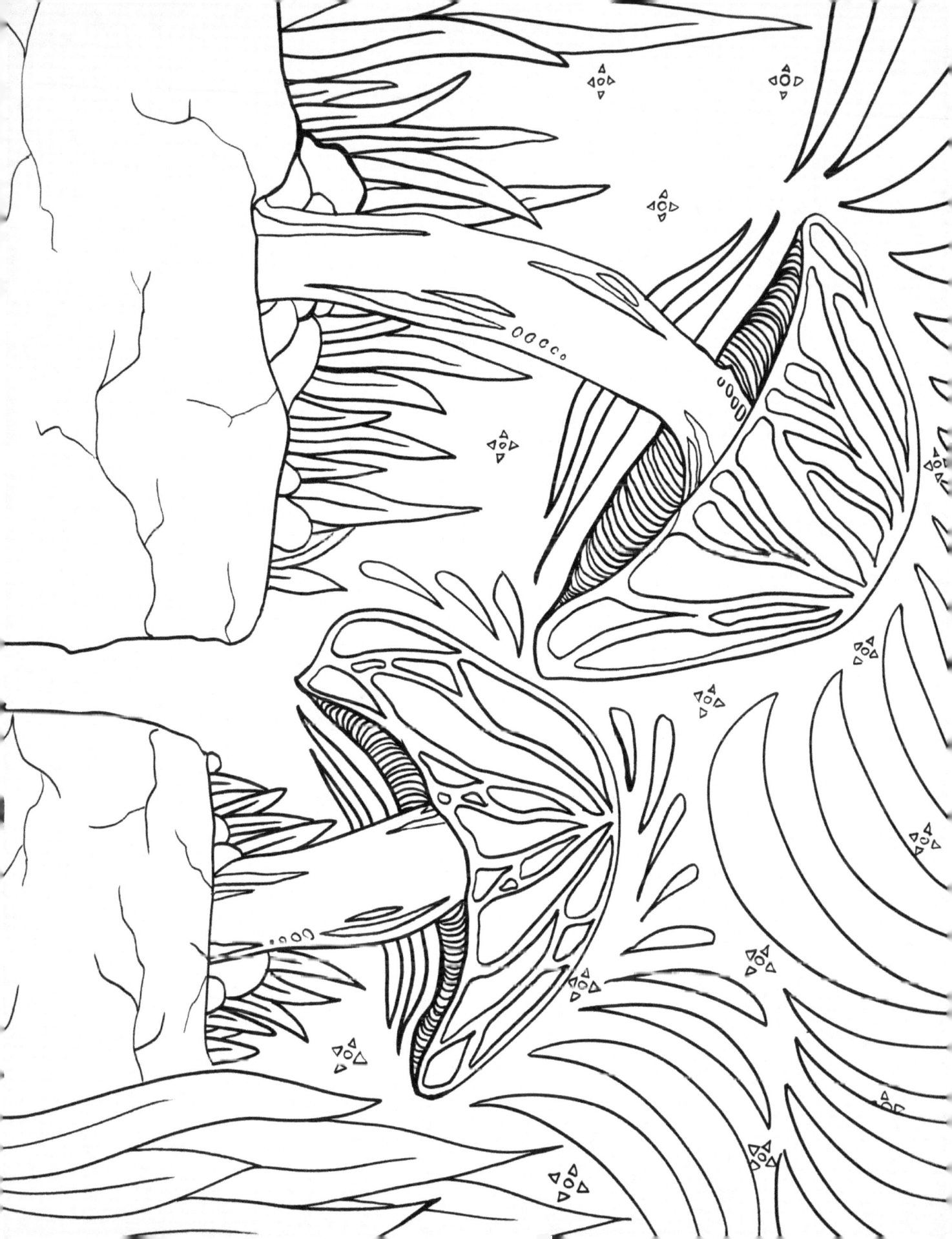

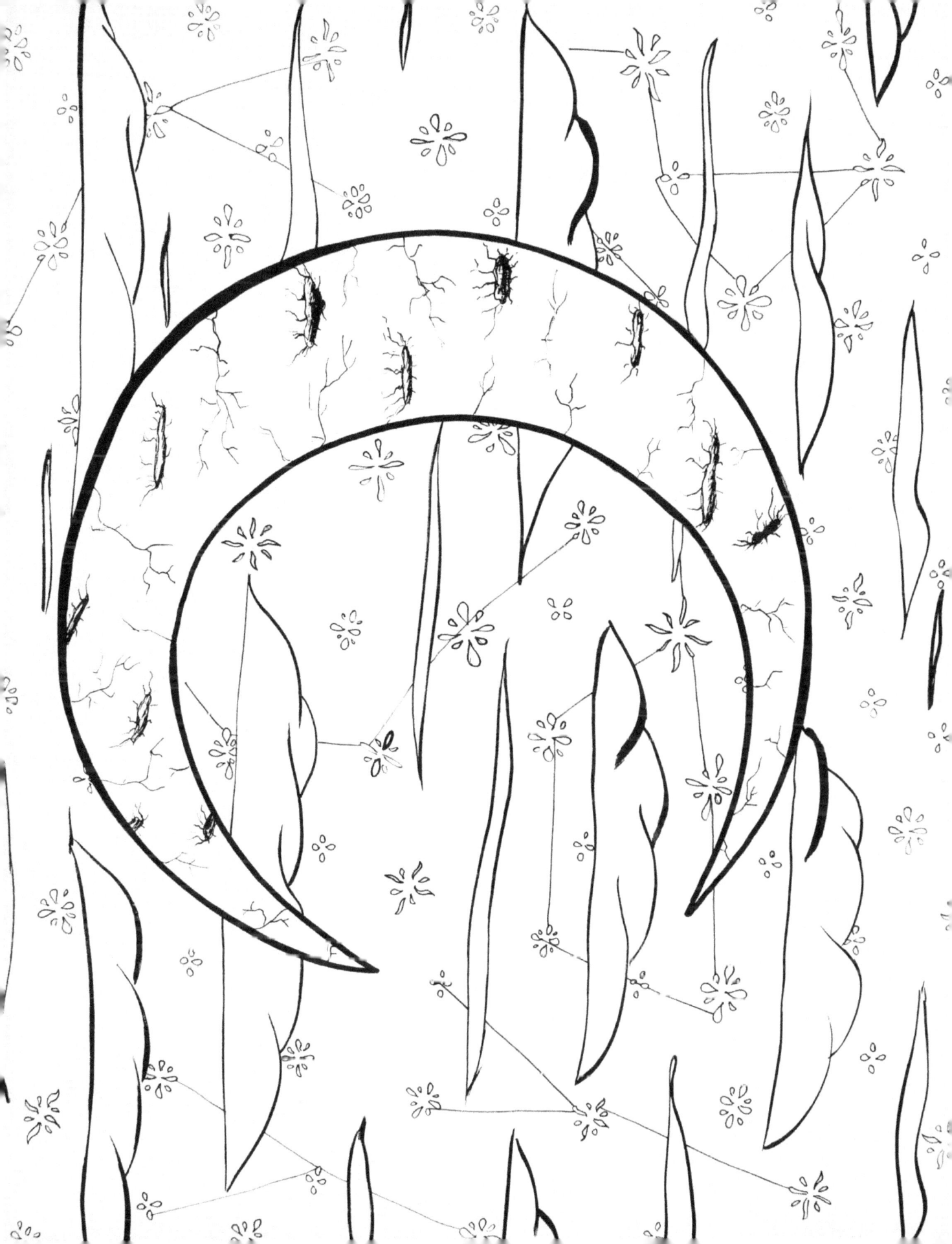

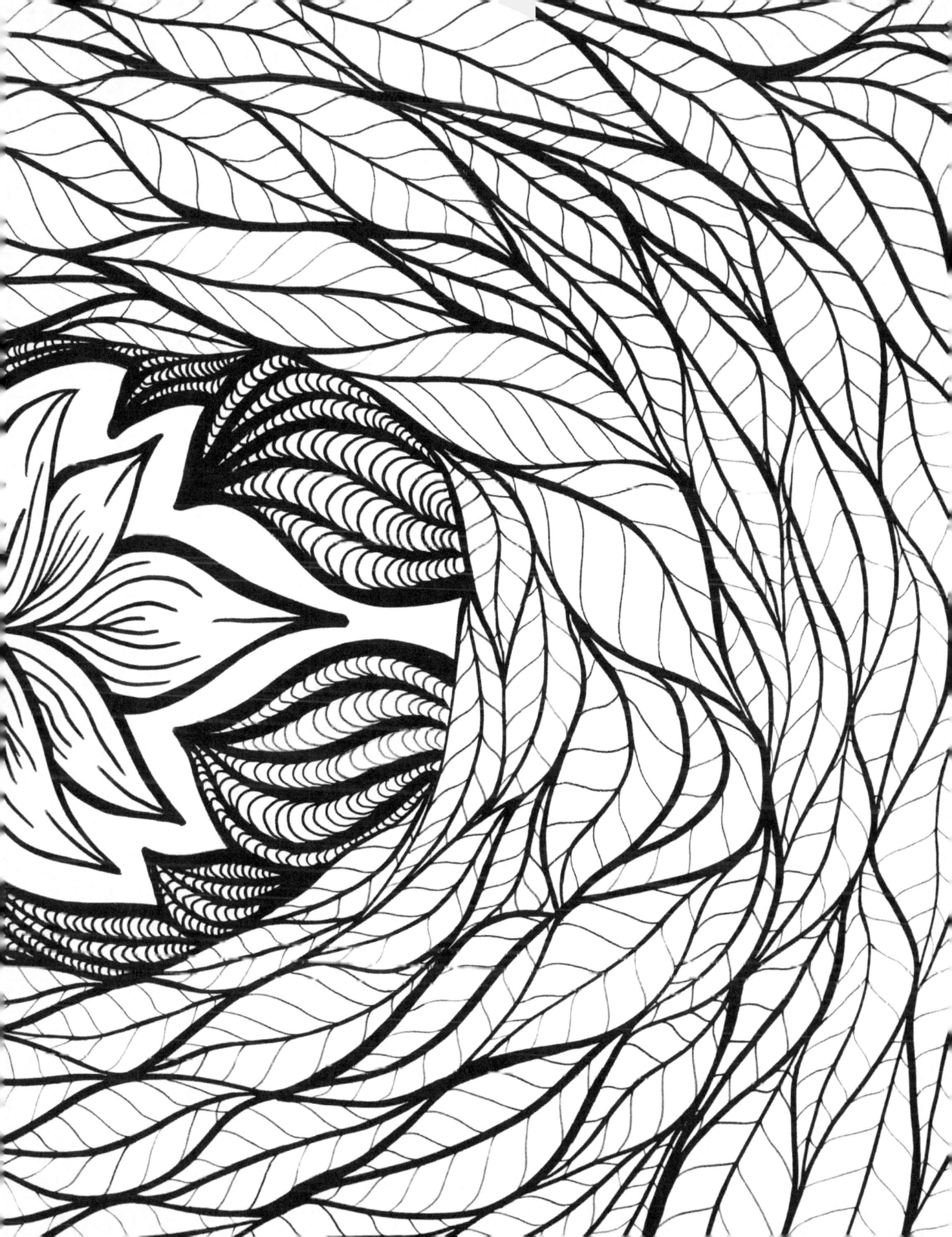

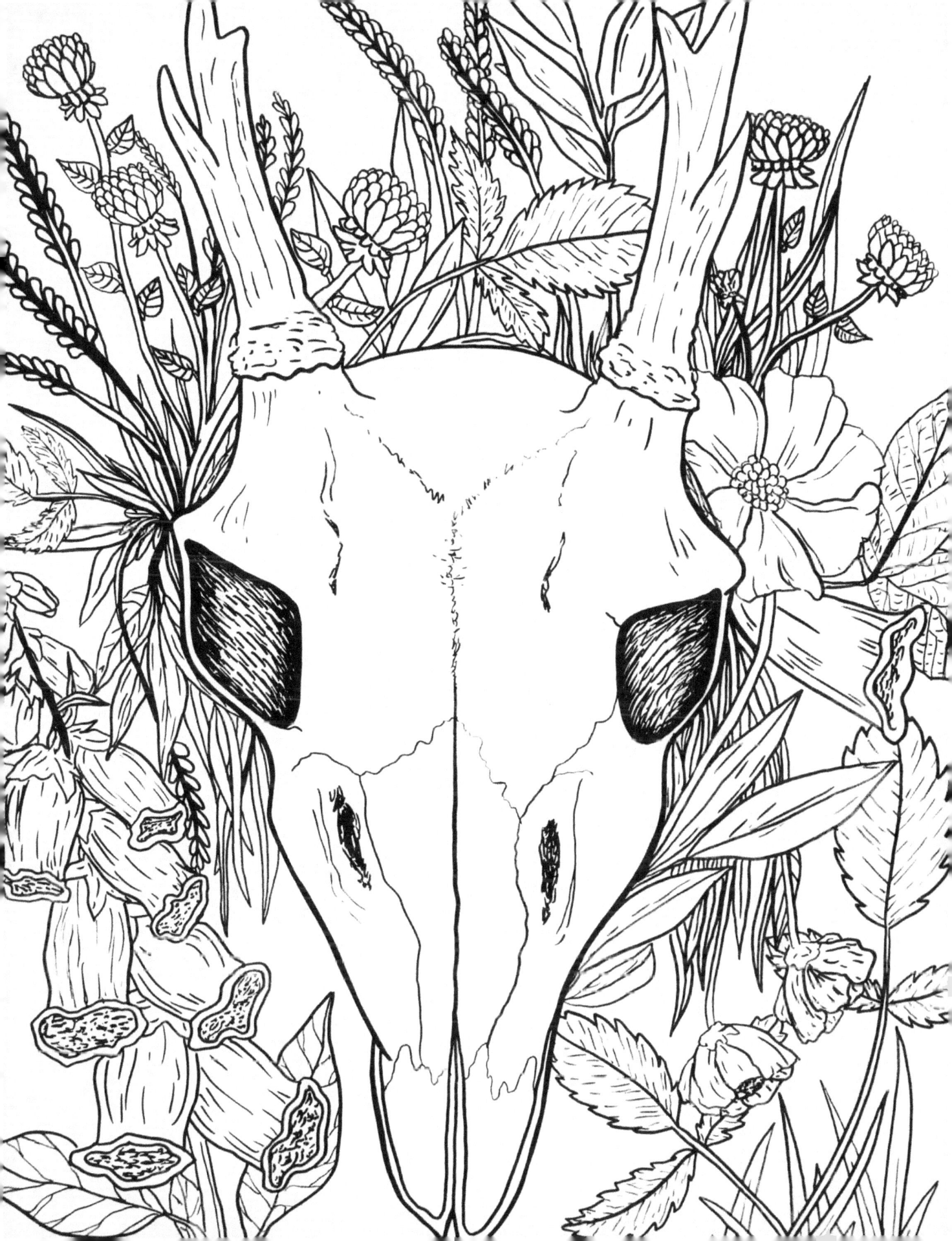

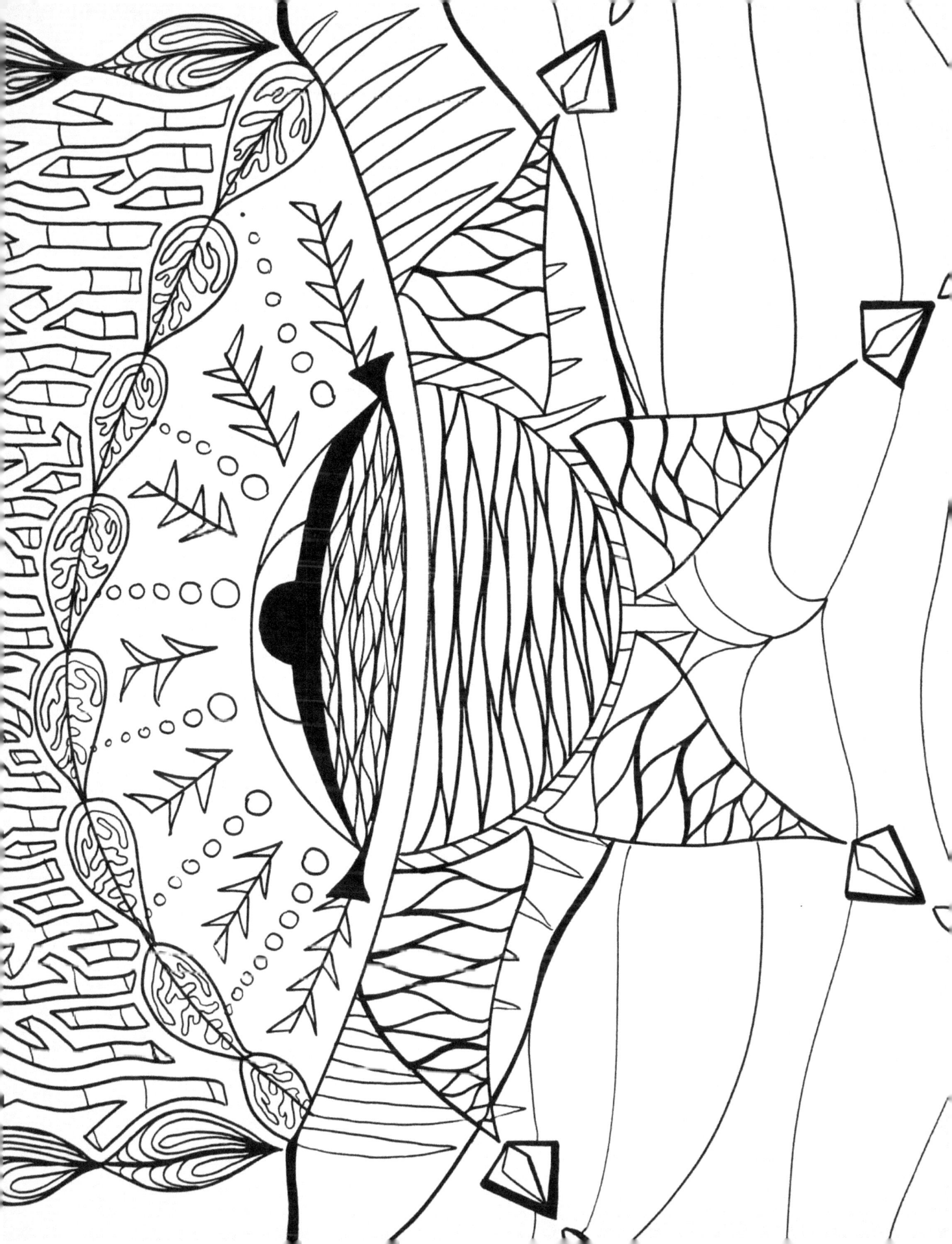

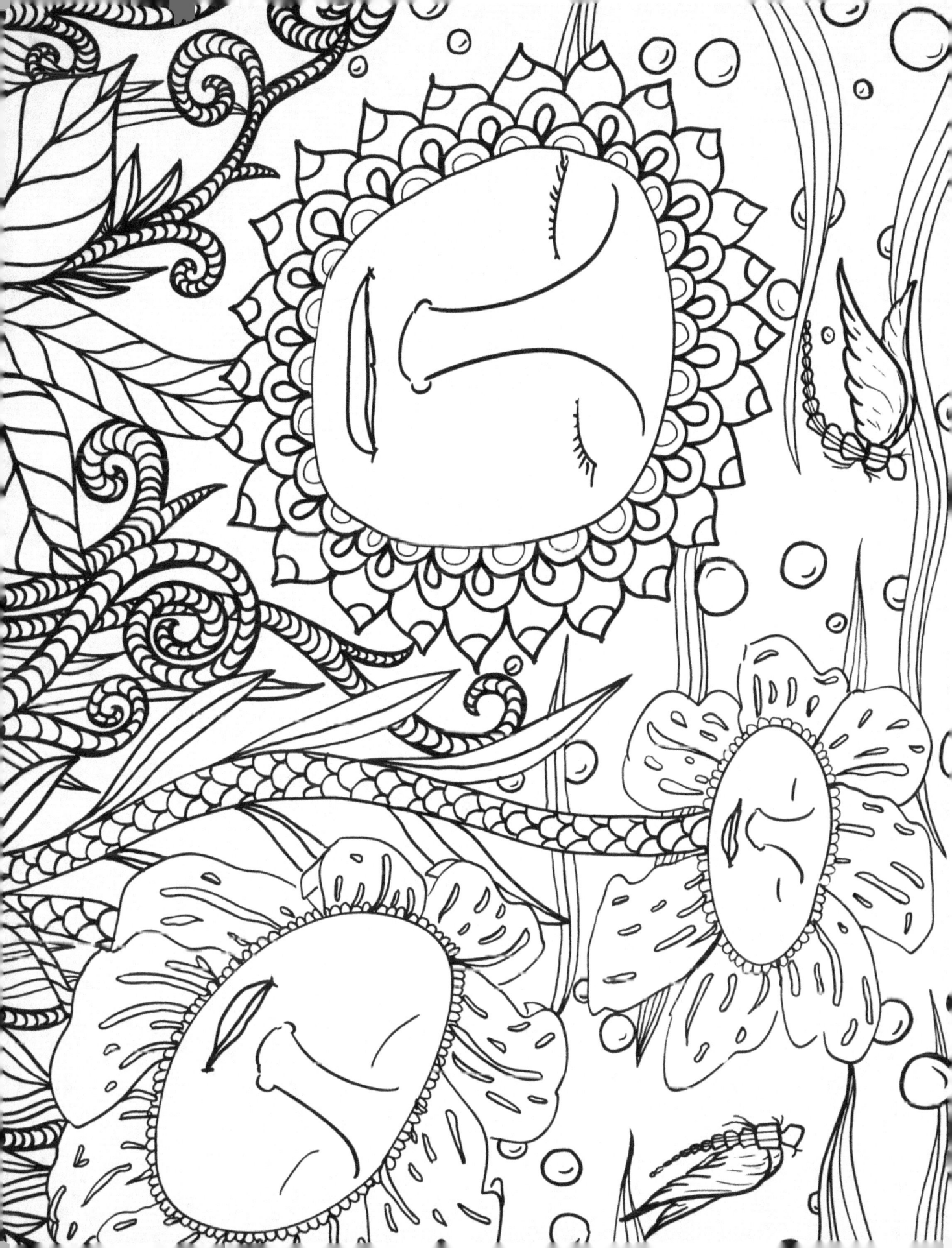

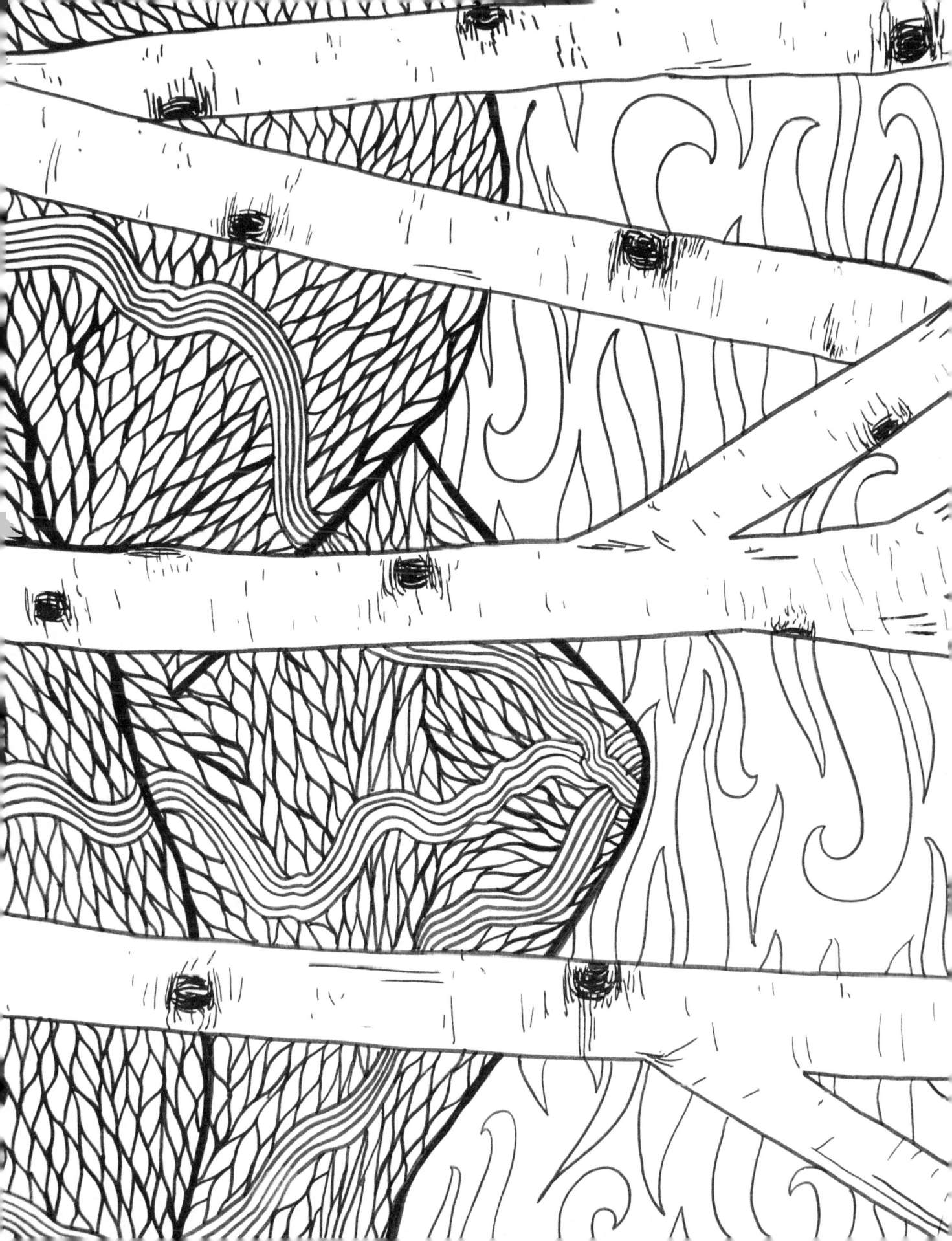

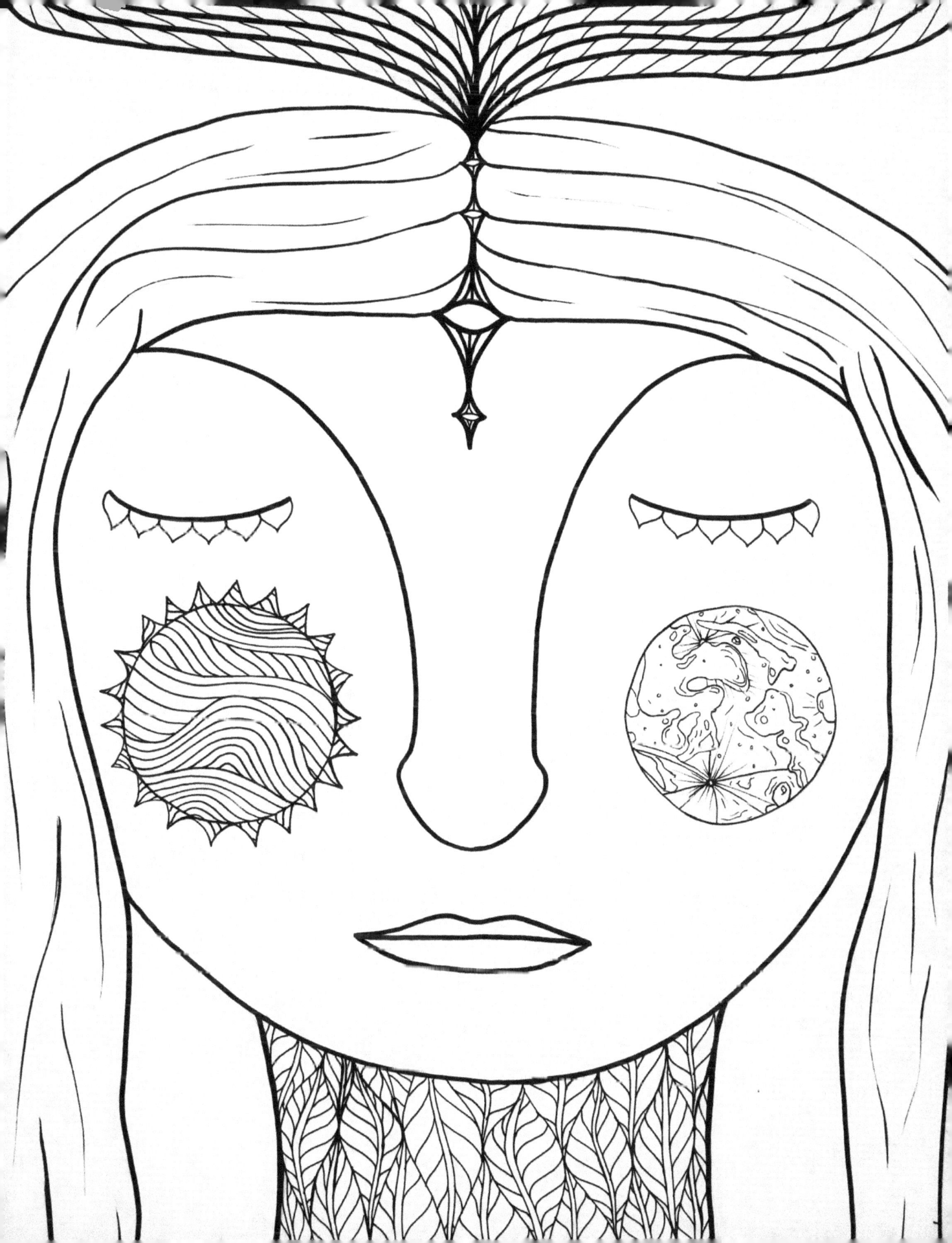

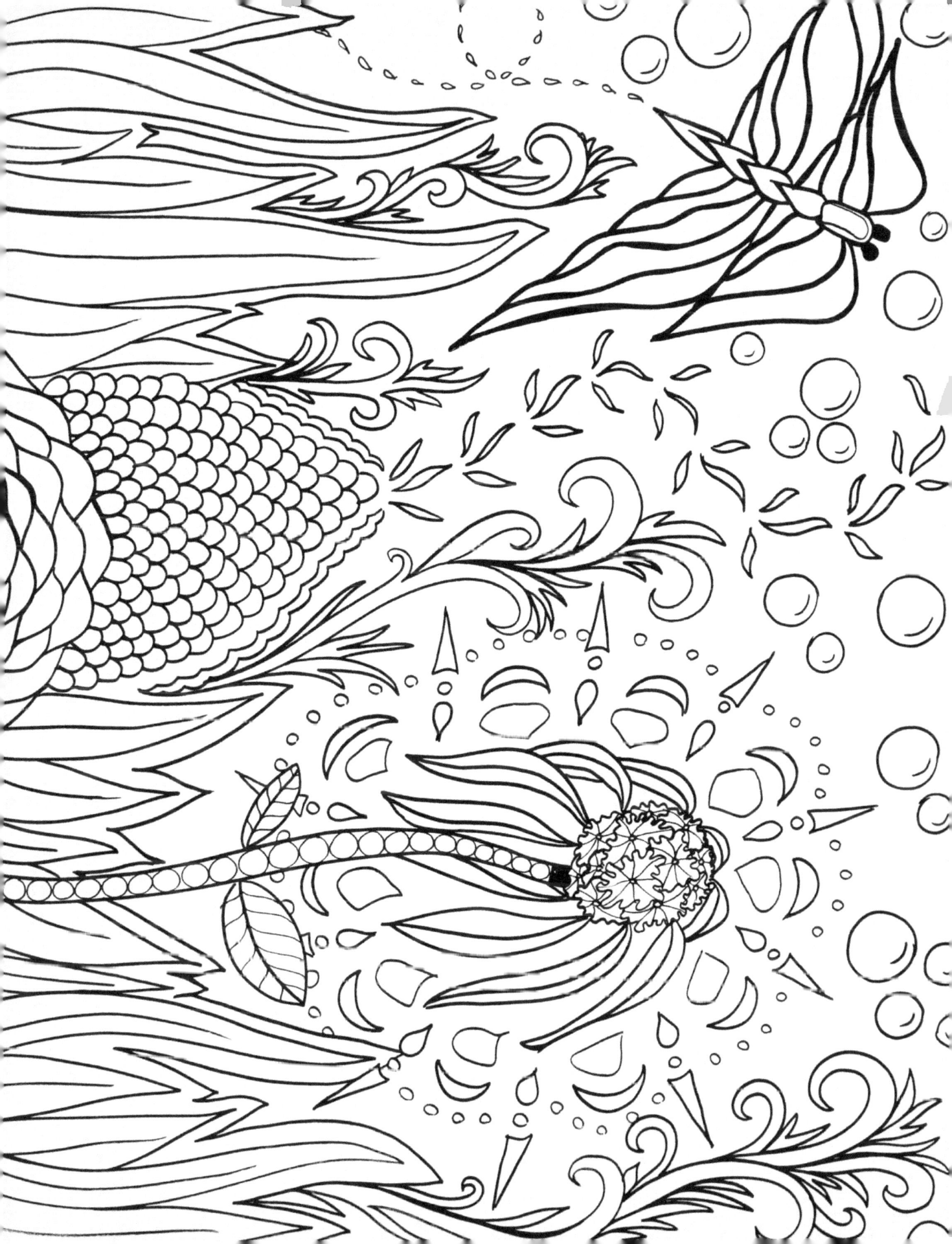

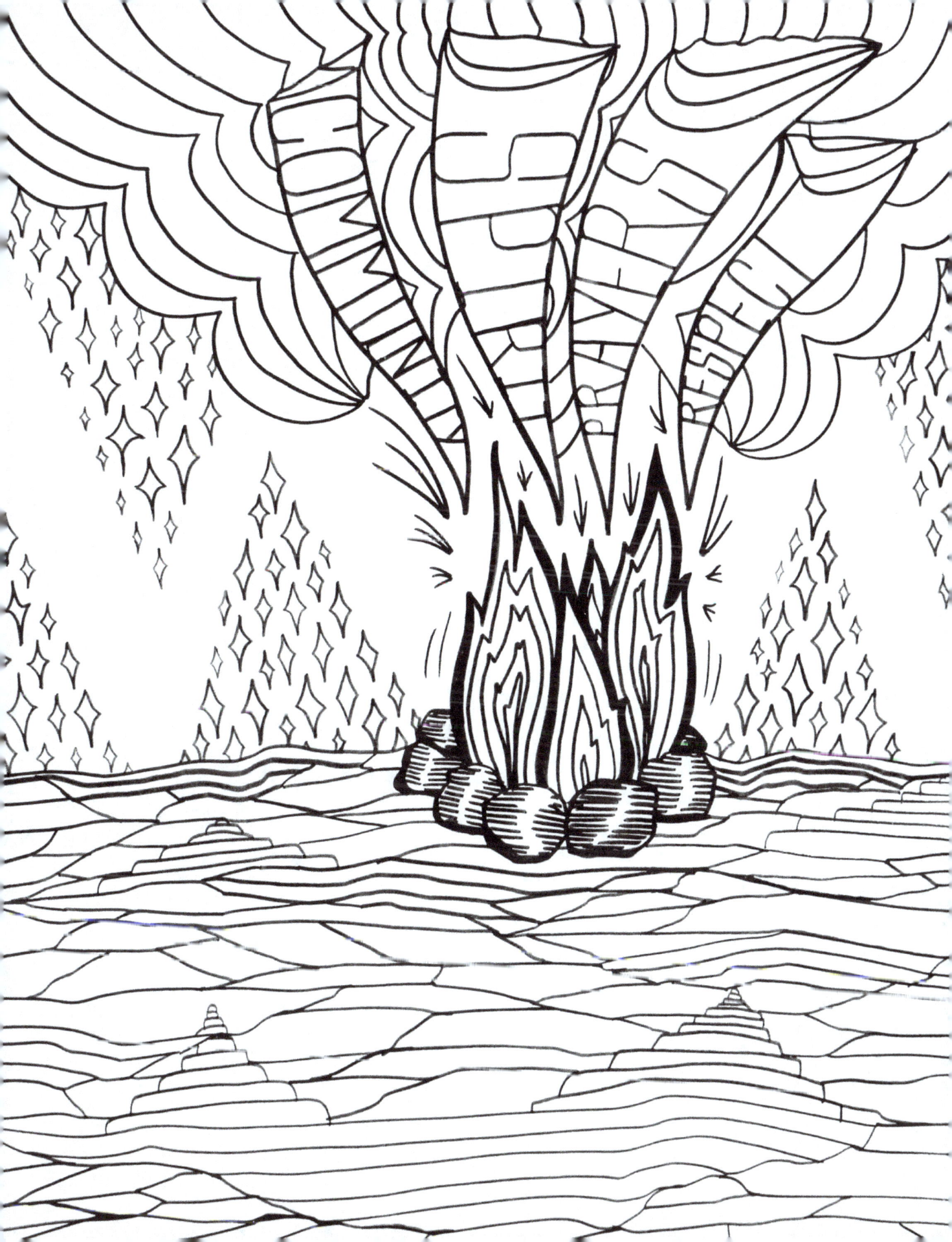

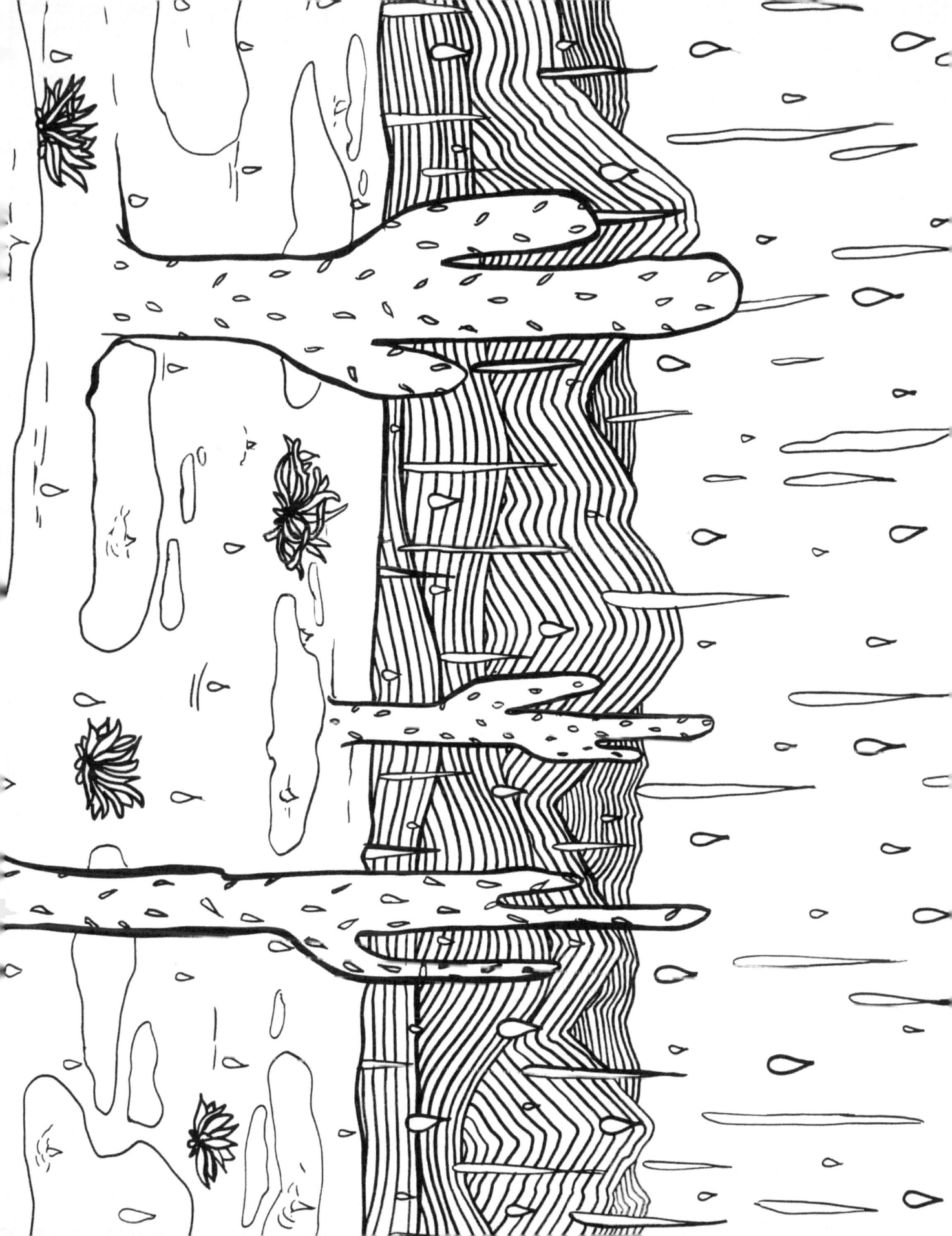

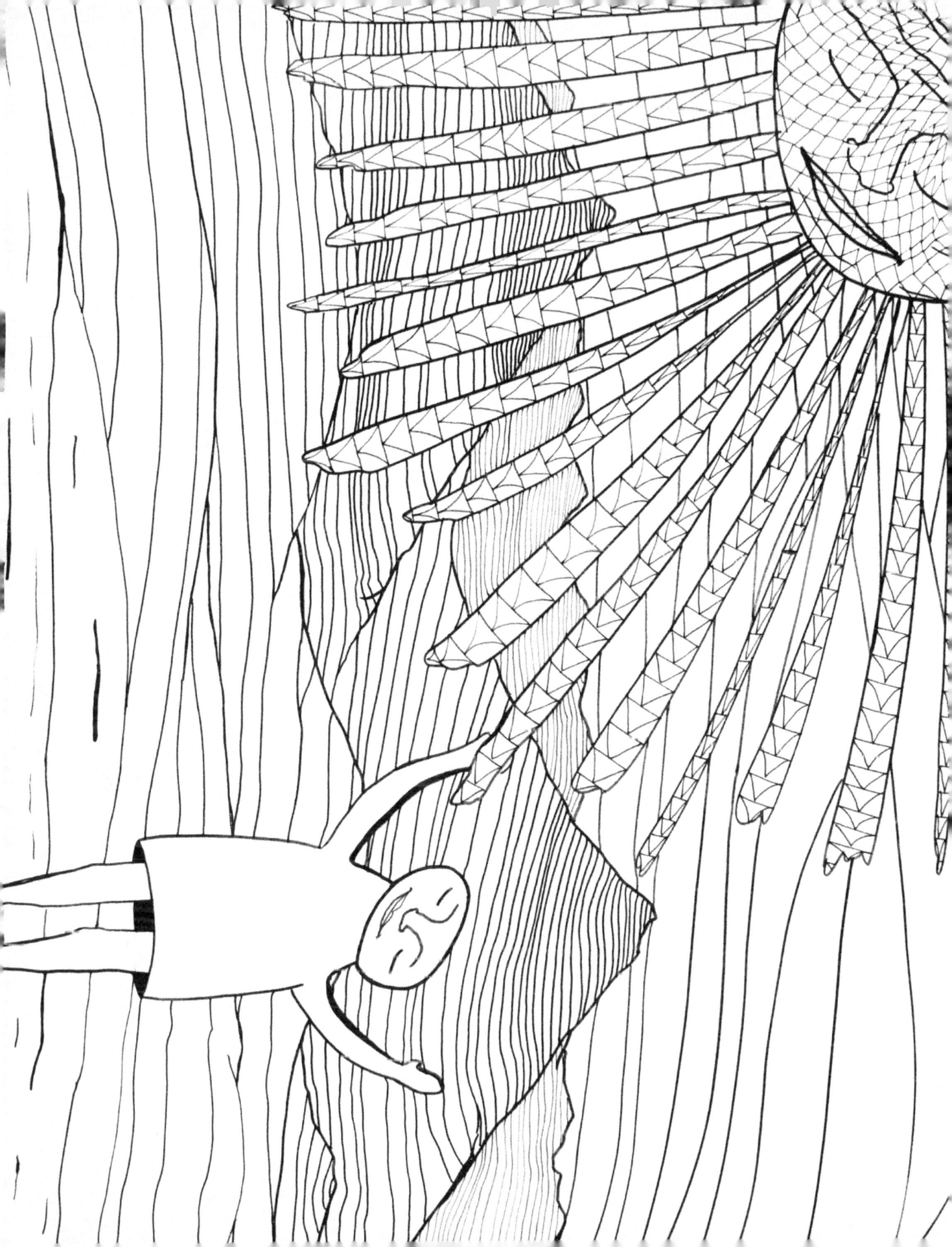

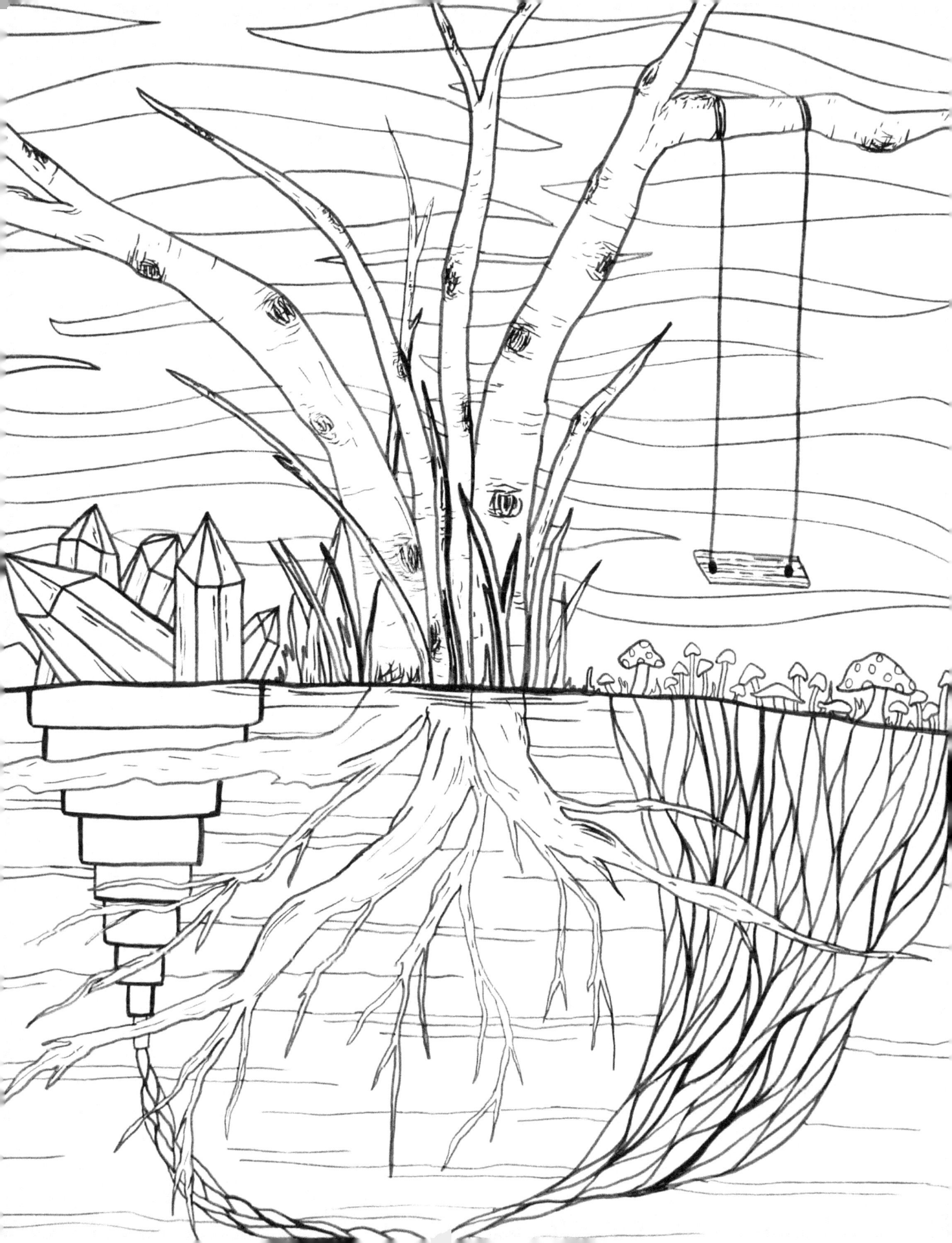

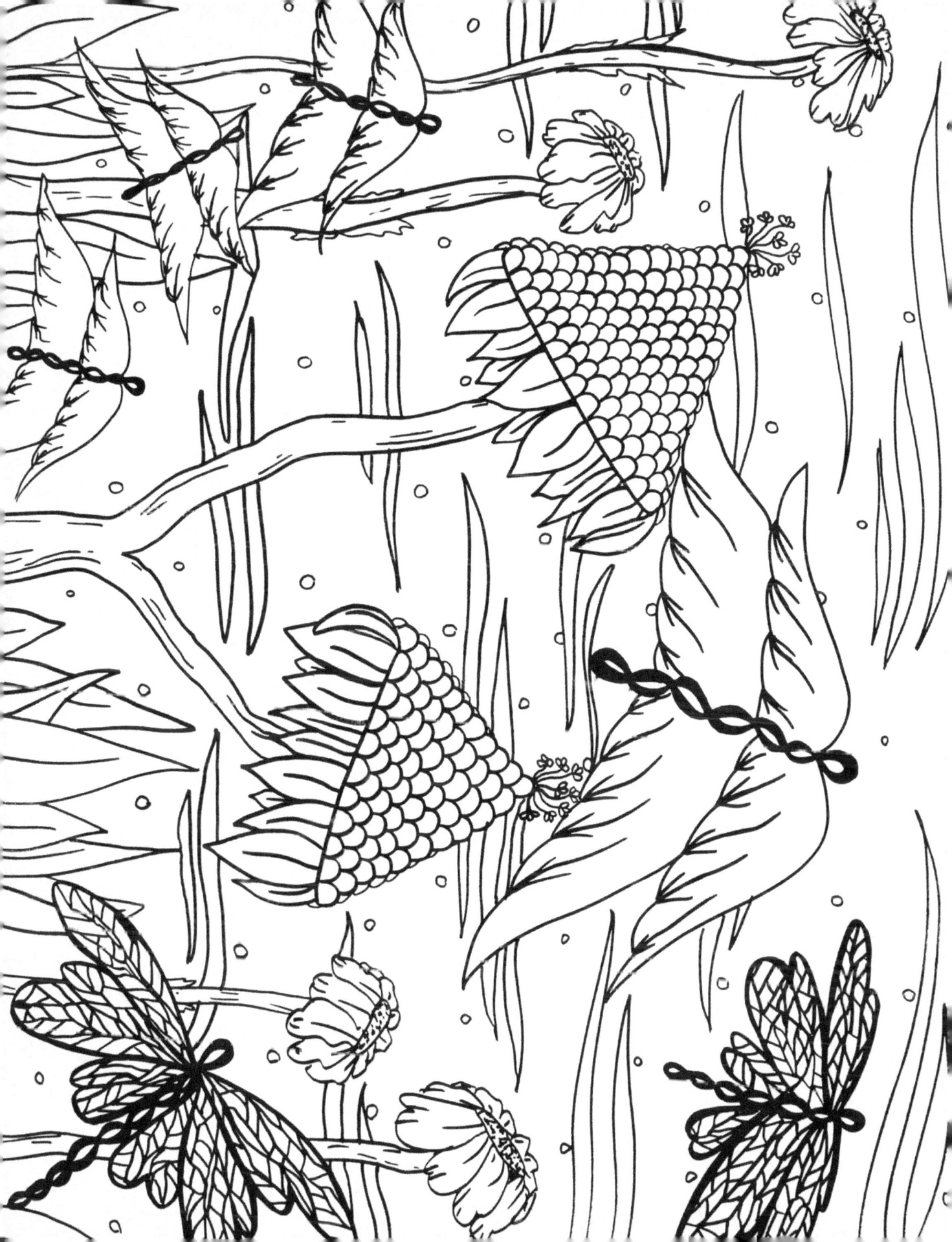

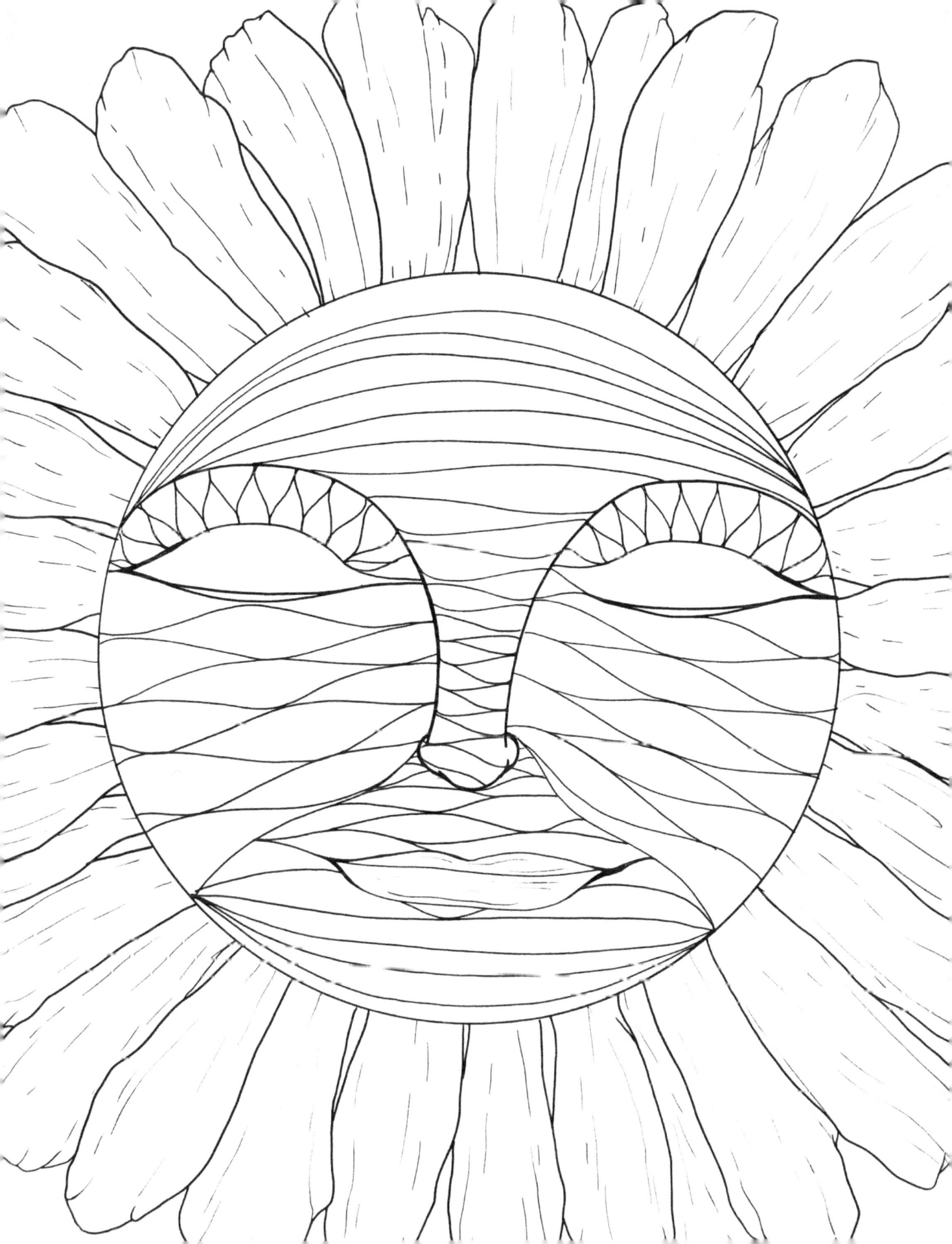

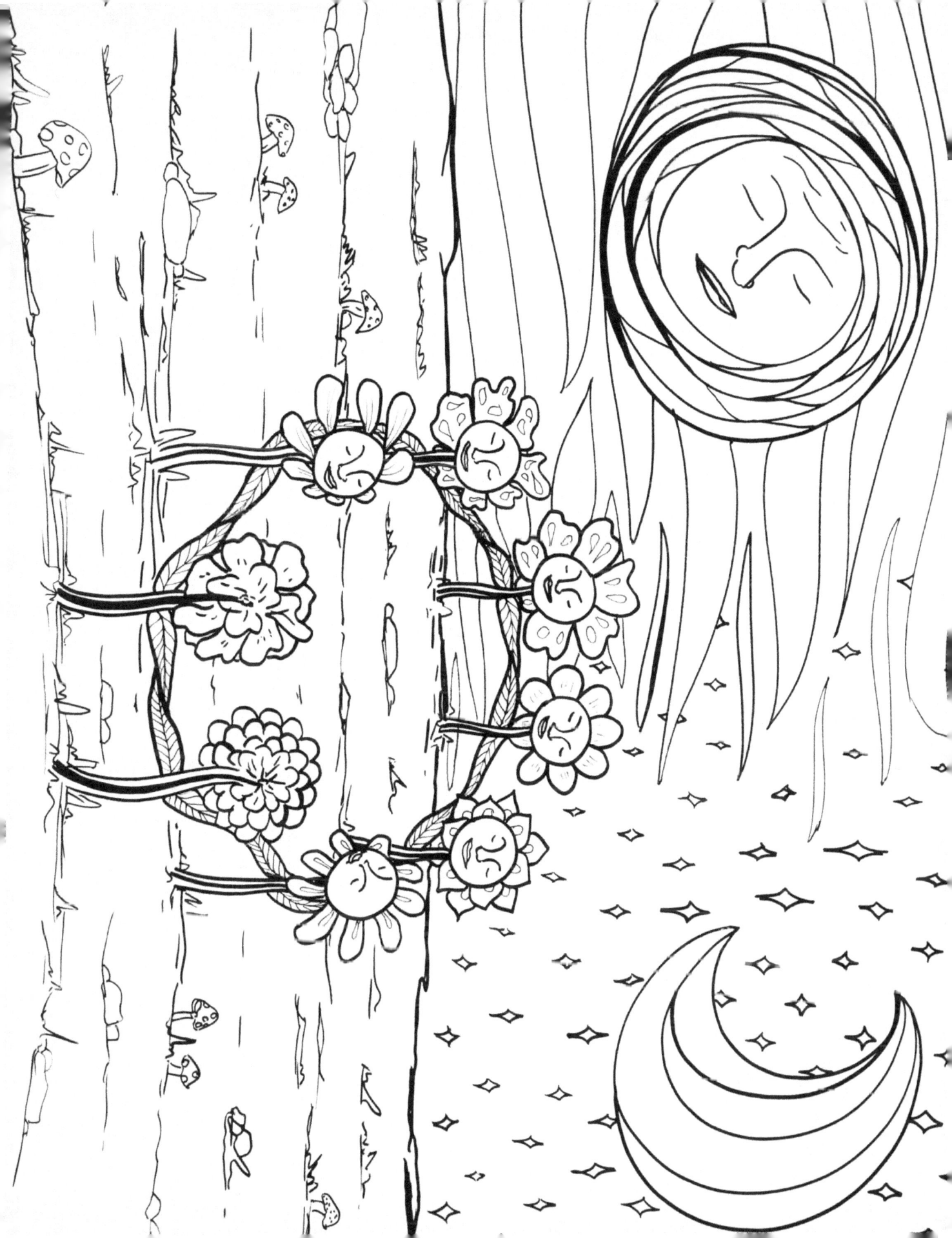

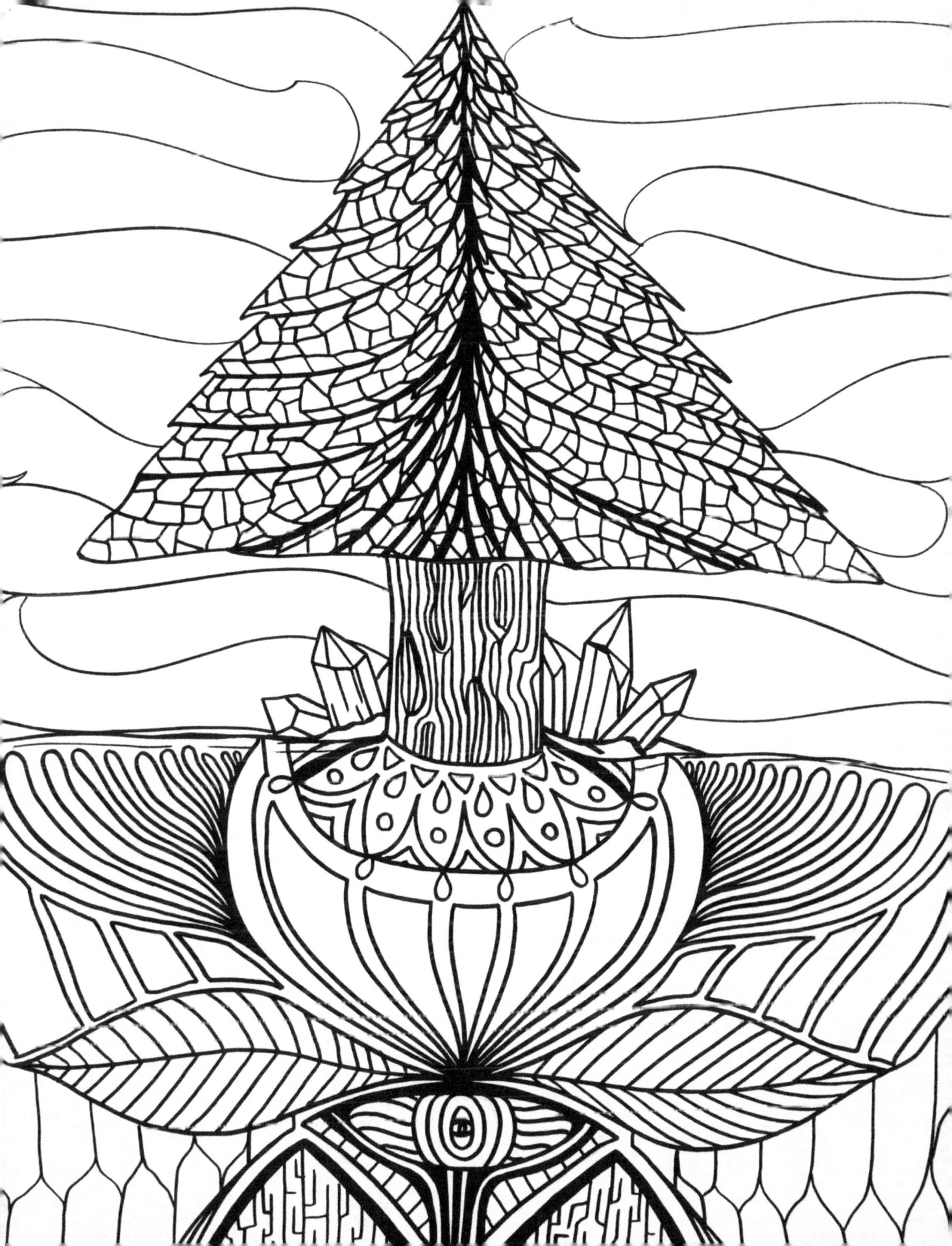

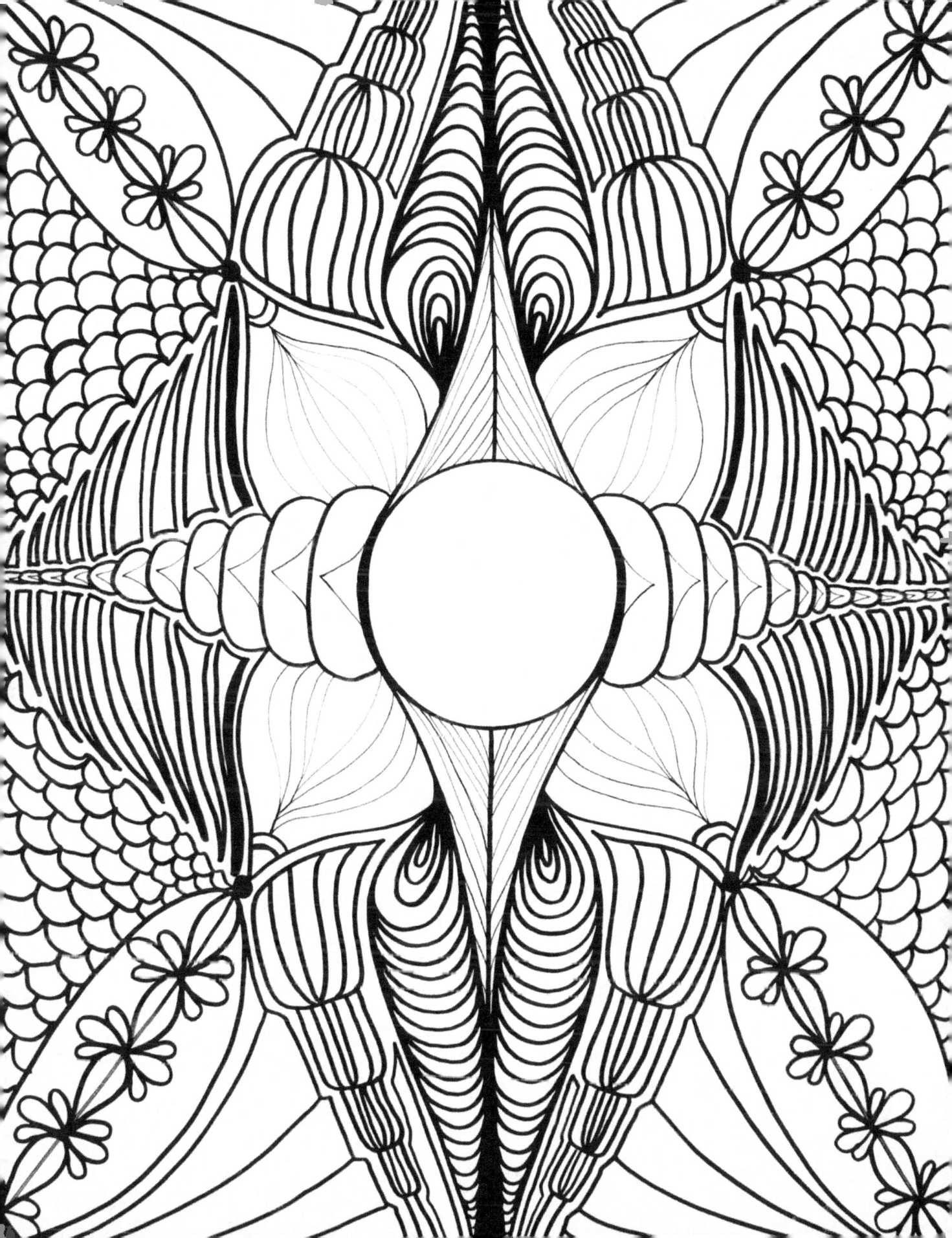

Journal

Journal

www.ingramcontent.com/pod-product-compliance
Lightning Source LLC
Chambersburg PA
CBHW081133180526
45170CB00008B/3087